MOJANG

THE NETHER & THE END
STICKER BOOK

EGMONT
We bring stories to life

First published in Great Britain 2018 by Egmont UK Limited
2 Minster Court, 10th floor, London EC3R 7BB

Written by Stephanie Milton
Designed by Joe Bolder and Ryan Gale
Illustrations by Ryan Marsh
Cover by Joe Bolder
Production by Laura Grundy and Louis Harvey
Special thanks to Lydia Winters, Owen Jones, Junkboy,
Martin Johansson, Marsh Davies and Jesper Oqvist.

MOJANG

ISBN 978 1 4052 9032 6

67871/009
Printed in China

Spending time online is great fun! Here are a few simple rules to help younger fans stay safe and keep the internet a great place to spend time:
- Never give out your real name – don't use it as your username.
- Never give out any of your personal details.
- Never tell anybody which school you go to or how old you are.
- Never tell anybody your password except a parent or a guardian.
- Be aware that you must be 13 or over to create an account on many sites. Always check the site
policy and ask a parent or guardian for permission before registering.
- Always tell a parent or guardian if something is worrying you.

Stay safe online. Any website addresses listed in this book are correct at the time of going to print. However, Egmont is not responsible for content hosted by third parties. Please be aware that online content can be subject to change and websites can contain content that is unsuitable for children. We advise that all children are supervised when using the internet.

NETHER EQUIPMENT

SURVIVAL
WITH BEAR

Psst! I hear you're thinking about visiting the Nether?
Listen closely – you're going to need all the help you can get.

A true survivor always has the right equipment for the job. Find some armour to wear, then craft some items to protect yourself.

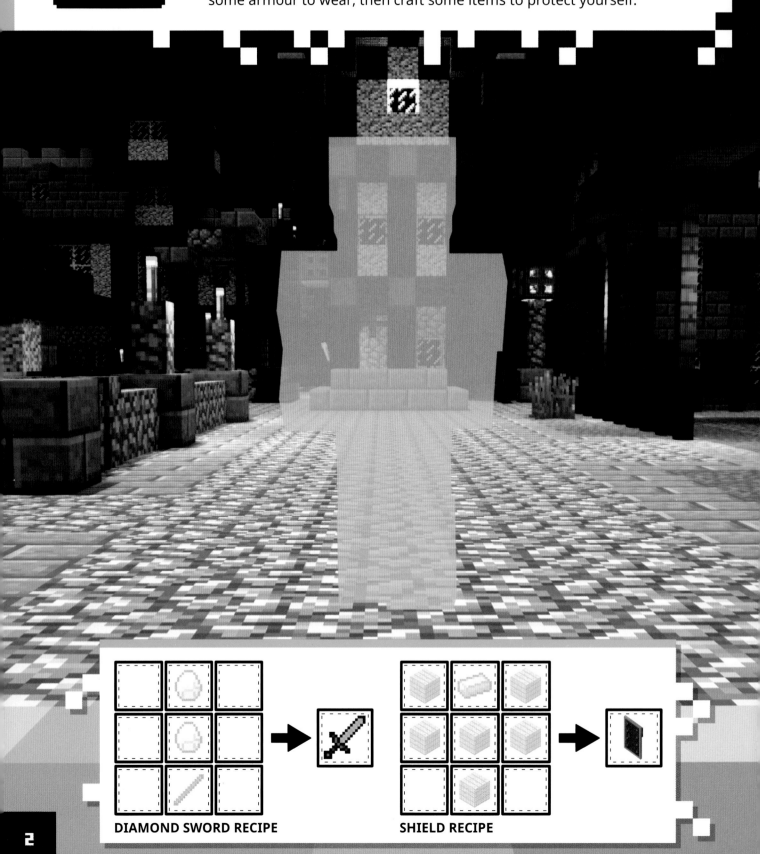

DIAMOND SWORD RECIPE

SHIELD RECIPE

NETHER PORTAL

Oh hey! Do you need some help building a Nether portal?
I just love building!

Find some obsidian block stickers on your sticker sheet, then
finish constructing the Nether portal.

BUILDING
WITH SPARKS

NETHER PORTAL

Nether portals allow you to travel from
the Overworld to the Nether. You'll need
at least 10 blocks of obsidian to build
one and it must be at least 4 x 5 blocks
in size, but you can leave the corners
out. Once the portal is built, activate it
with a flint and steel, then step through.

NETHER MOBS

COMBAT
WITH SCOUT

If you're looking for advice about how to deal with the Nether's mobs, you've come to the right person – I've faced these monsters many times and lived to tell the tale.

Find the sticker for each mob info card to learn all about them.

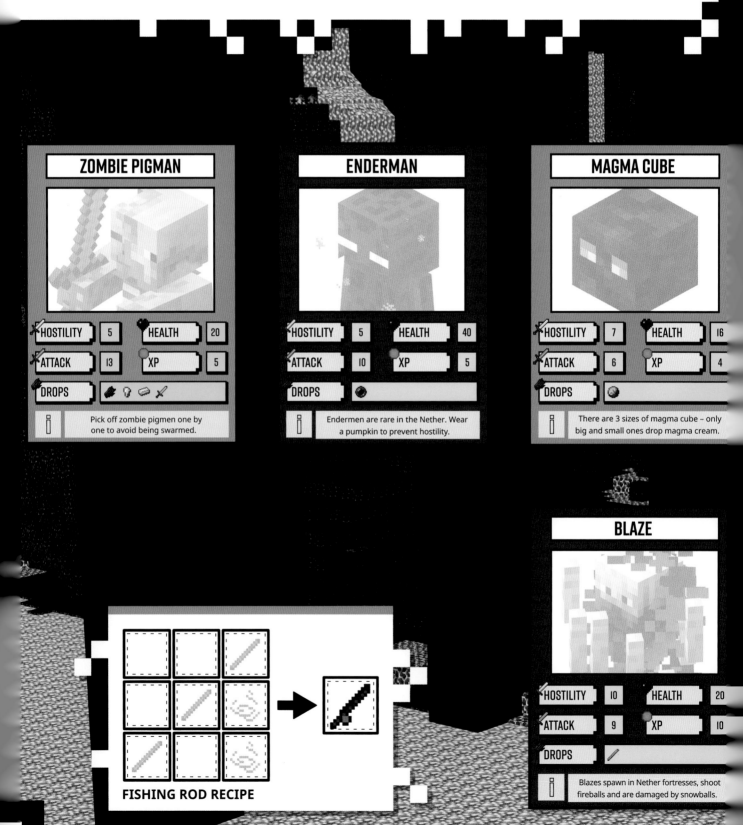

ZOMBIE PIGMAN

HOSTILITY	5	HEALTH	20
ATTACK	13	XP	5
DROPS			

ℹ Pick off zombie pigmen one by one to avoid being swarmed.

ENDERMAN

HOSTILITY	5	HEALTH	40
ATTACK	10	XP	5
DROPS			

ℹ Endermen are rare in the Nether. Wear a pumpkin to prevent hostility.

MAGMA CUBE

HOSTILITY	7	HEALTH	16
ATTACK	6	XP	4
DROPS			

ℹ There are 3 sizes of magma cube – only big and small ones drop magma cream.

BLAZE

HOSTILITY	10	HEALTH	20
ATTACK	9	XP	10
DROPS			

ℹ Blazes spawn in Nether fortresses, shoot fireballs and are damaged by snowballs.

FISHING ROD RECIPE

GHAST

HOSTILITY	10	HEALTH	10
ATTACK	25	XP	5
DROPS			

Ghasts are fierce foes. Reel one in with a fishing rod then attack it with a sword.

SKELETON

HOSTILITY	7	HEALTH	20
ATTACK	5	XP	5
DROPS			

Skeletons are a common mob, but only occasionally pop up in Nether fortresses.

WITHER SKELETON

HOSTILITY	9	HEALTH	20
ATTACK	10	XP	5
DROPS			

Wither skeletons drop their skull, which is needed to summon the wither boss mob.

SNOWBALLS

Snowballs can be obtained when you break a snow block with a shovel.

A TERRIBLE FORTRESS

Good day! Care to explore this magnificent fortress with me? No doubt there'll be some wonderful discoveries waiting for us inside!

Navigate the maze to find the exit, picking up loot as you go. Do try to avoid the mobs, though – they don't look very friendly ...

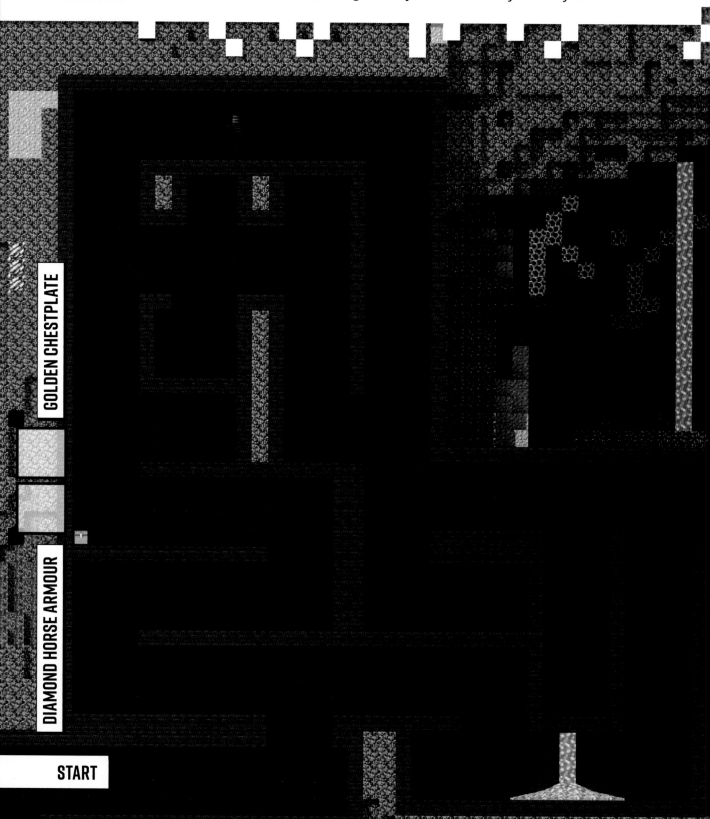

GOLDEN CHESTPLATE

DIAMOND HORSE ARMOUR

START

GOLDEN SWORD

IRON HORSE ARMOUR

FINISH

SADDLE

OBSIDIAN

NETHER WART

GHASTLY ENCOUNTER

SURVIVAL
WITH BEAR

You're crossing the Nether terrain when you hear a terrifying shriek. You look up and see a ghast. It may be the Nether's most dangerous mob, but if you keep calm and use your head you can escape in one piece.

Use stickers from your sticker sheet to complete the story.

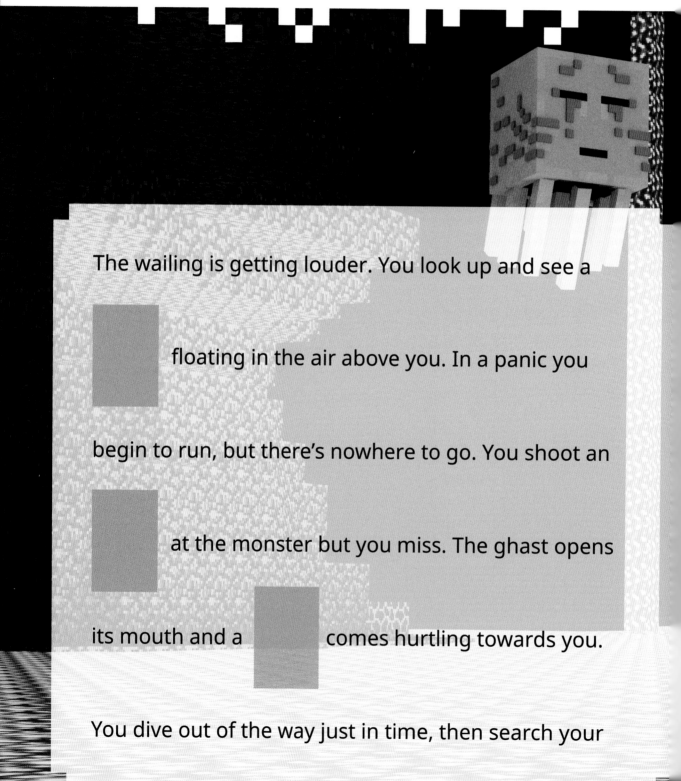

The wailing is getting louder. You look up and see a

floating in the air above you. In a panic you

begin to run, but there's nowhere to go. You shoot an

at the monster but you miss. The ghast opens

its mouth and a   comes hurtling towards you.

You dive out of the way just in time, then search your

inventory to find some 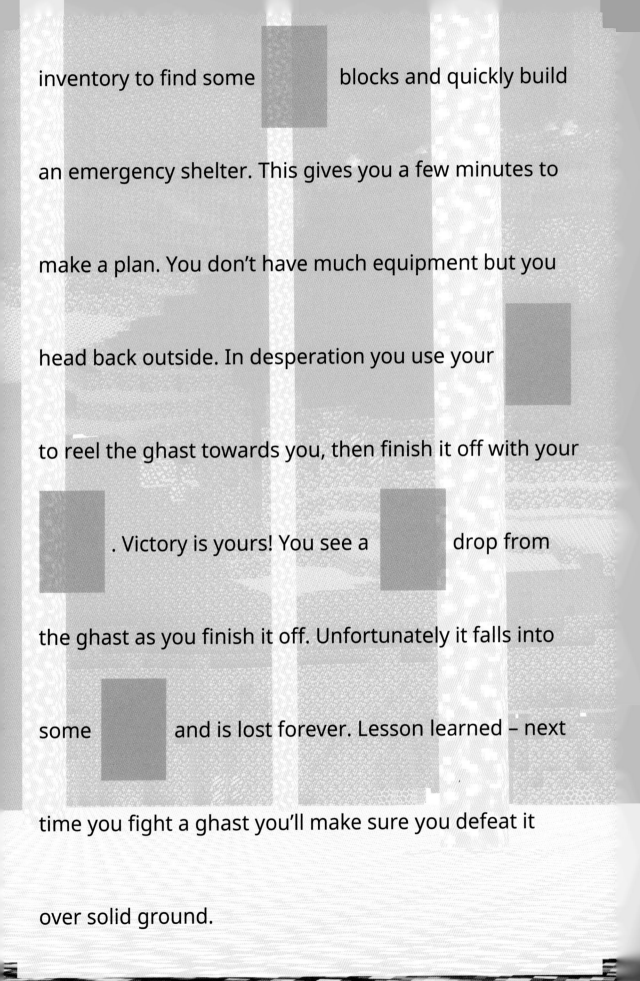 blocks and quickly build

an emergency shelter. This gives you a few minutes to

make a plan. You don't have much equipment but you

head back outside. In desperation you use your

to reel the ghast towards you, then finish it off with your

. Victory is yours! You see a drop from

the ghast as you finish it off. Unfortunately it falls into

some and is lost forever. Lesson learned – next

time you fight a ghast you'll make sure you defeat it

over solid ground.

TAKING SHELTER

Isn't being in the Nether super fun? It's so orange and burny! It can't hurt to find somewhere to take shelter, though, just in case you find yourself in a spot of trouble ...

Let's repair and seal off a section of the fortress with Nether brick. And while you're in there, why not light it up with glowstone?

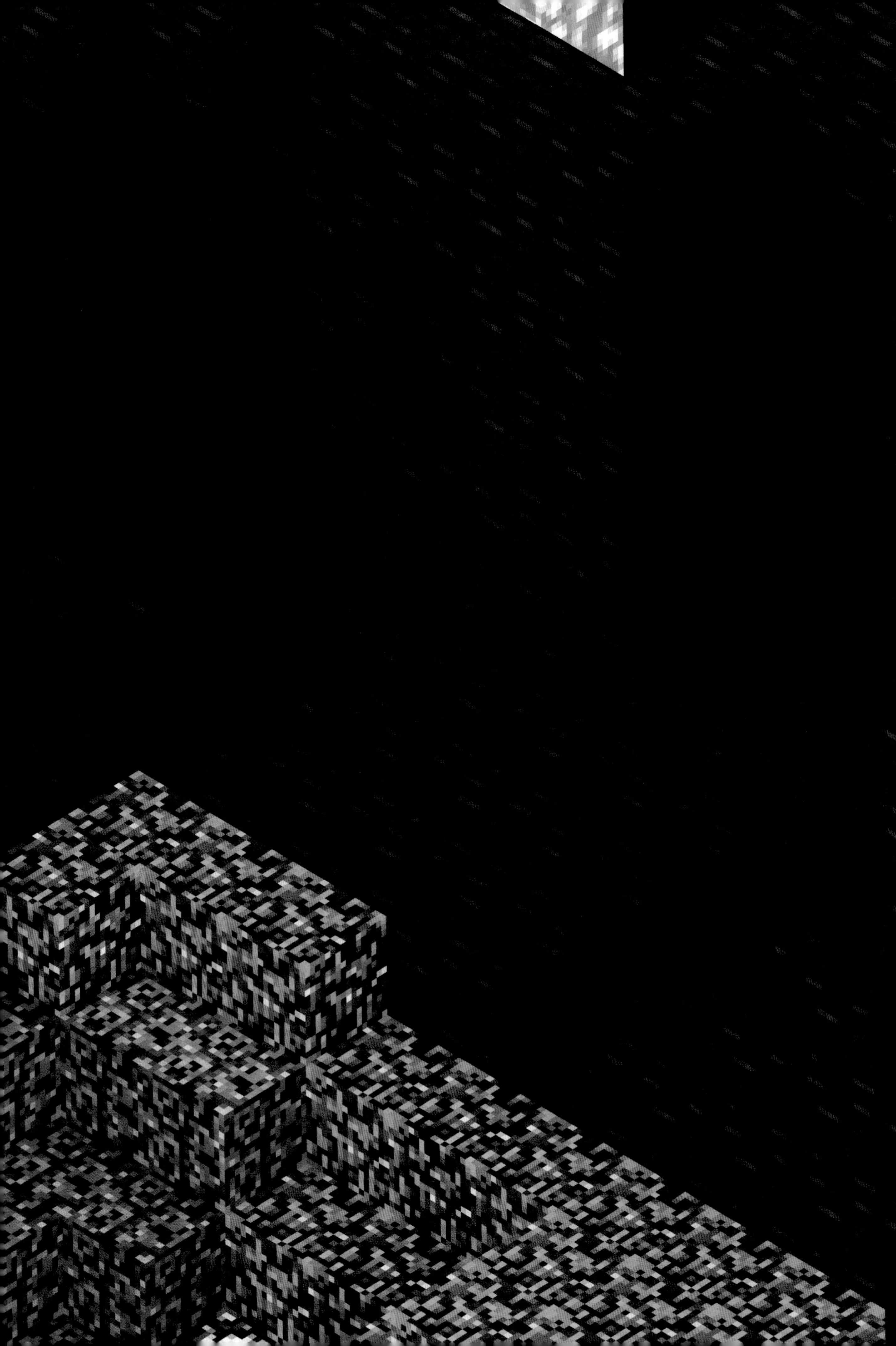

CRAFTING
WITH SPARKS

NETHER LOOT

Now you're safely back in the Overworld you can take a proper look at all the Nether loot you collected and discover what it can be used for.
I just love new crafting recipes!

Read the clue next to each item, then find the correct sticker for the box.

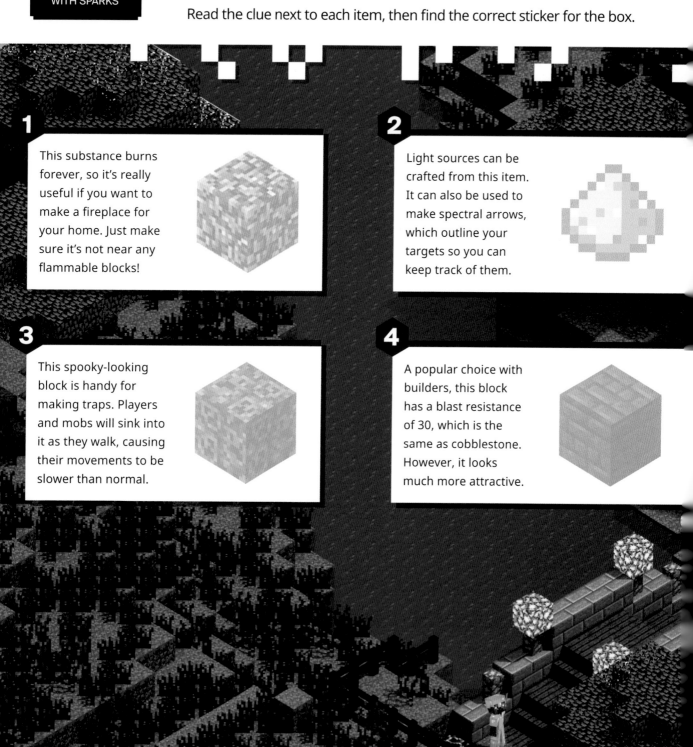

1

This substance burns forever, so it's really useful if you want to make a fireplace for your home. Just make sure it's not near any flammable blocks!

2

Light sources can be crafted from this item. It can also be used to make spectral arrows, which outline your targets so you can keep track of them.

3

This spooky-looking block is handy for making traps. Players and mobs will sink into it as they walk, causing their movements to be slower than normal.

4

A popular choice with builders, this block has a blast resistance of 30, which is the same as cobblestone. However, it looks much more attractive.

5

This block is handy for making traps, as it deals fire damage. It's useless in the Nether, though, as the native mobs are immune to fire damage.

6

You can use this substance to craft several useful redstone items. It can also be combined to make several kinds of decorative blocks.

THE WITHER

Do you have the guts to take on the terrifying wither? While you think about that, let me share some of my pro tips with you.

Finish building the wither to bring it to life, then complete the recipes to help you defeat it.

POTION OF STRENGTH

Drink a potion of strength and you'll be able to do more damage to the wither with your sword.

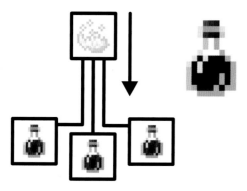

POTION OF STRENGTH RECIPE

POTION OF HEALING

Potion of healing helps you to heal, and it will also harm the wither if you brew it into a splash potion.

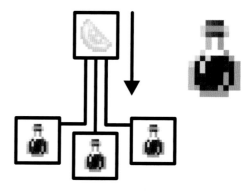

POTION OF HEALING RECIPE

SNOW GOLEM

A snow golem will distract the wither with its snowballs, giving you the chance to get some hits in. You can make a snow golem by placing a pumpkin on top of 2 blocks of snow.

NETHER STAR

The wither drops a Nether star when defeated. This rare item can be used to craft a beacon – a structure that provides helpful status effects when you're near it.

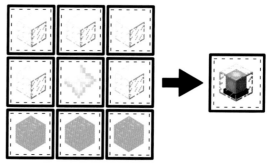

BEACON RECIPE

FOLLOW THE EYES

If you're as keen to visit the End dimension as I am, you'll need to find an End portal. They're hidden deep underground in strongholds, and you can find them by throwing eyes of ender.

Finish the eye of ender recipe using your stickers, then follow the coordinates to find the stronghold.

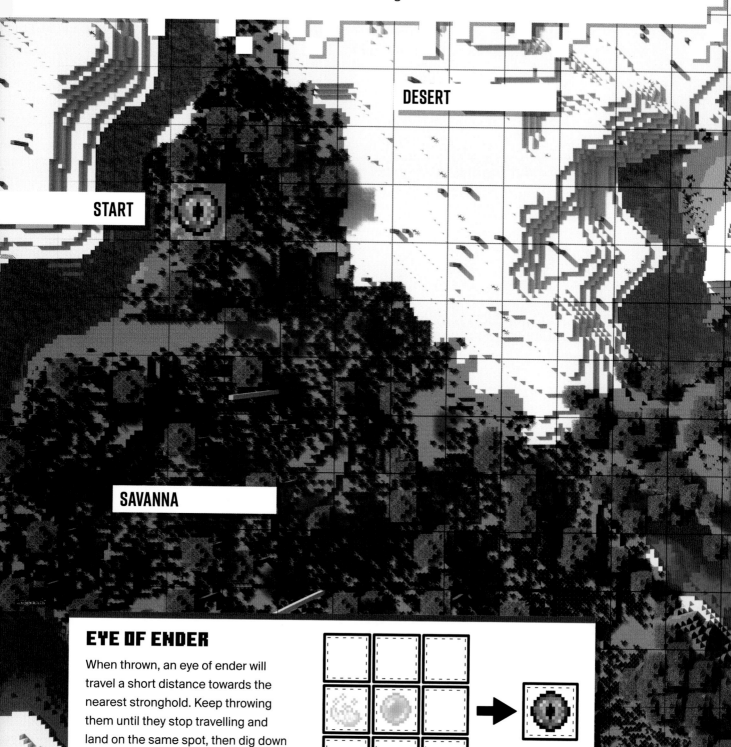

DESERT

START

SAVANNA

EYE OF ENDER

When thrown, an eye of ender will travel a short distance towards the nearest stronghold. Keep throwing them until they stop travelling and land on the same spot, then dig down to find the stronghold.

EYE OF ENDER RECIPE

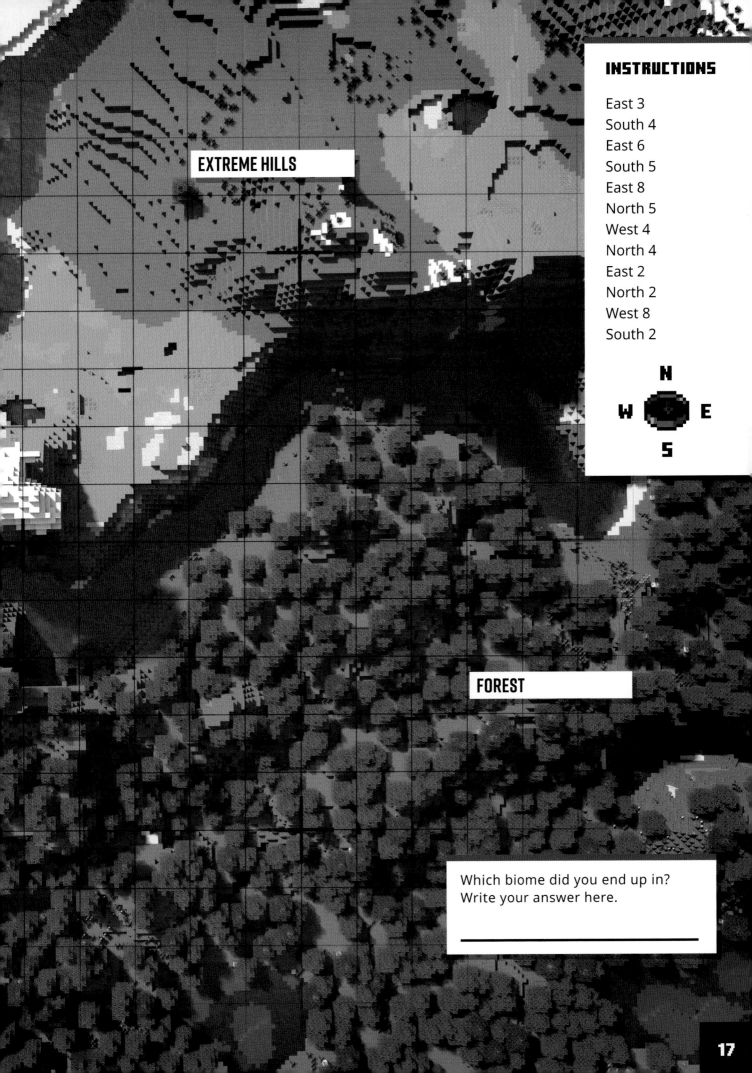

EXTREME HILLS

INSTRUCTIONS

East 3
South 4
East 6
South 5
East 8
North 5
West 4
North 4
East 2
North 2
West 8
South 2

FOREST

Which biome did you end up in?
Write your answer here.

_____

THE STRONGHOLD

SURVIVAL
WITH BEAR

The stronghold is a maze of corridors, and danger could be lurking around every corner. This is the perfect opportunity to work on your survival skills.

Find a path to the portal room, avoiding hostile mobs and lava and picking up loot along the way.

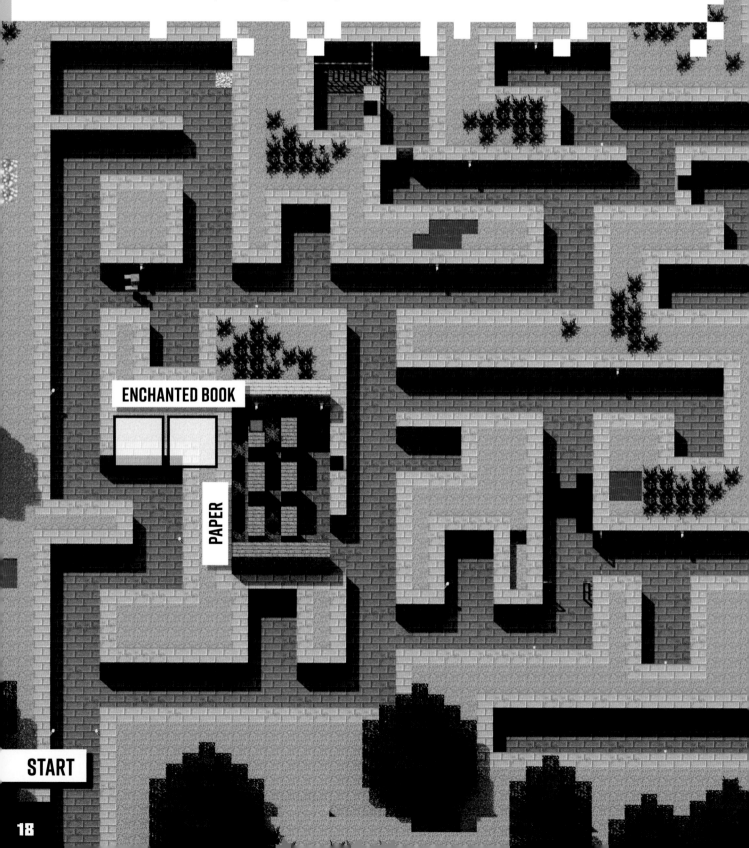

ENCHANTED BOOK

PAPER

START

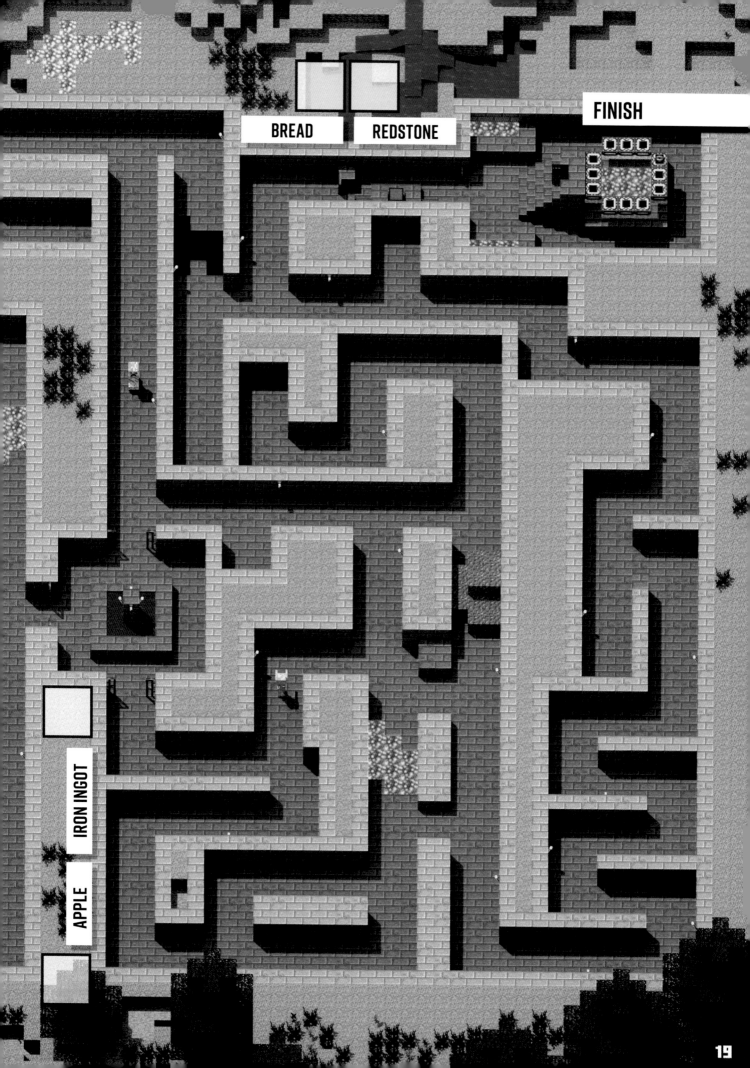

BREAD

REDSTONE

FINISH

IRON INGOT

APPLE

19

PORTAL ROOM

Oh gosh, you've finally reached the portal! This is so exciting! Burny lava is my favourite, and you're about to cross over to the End dimension! Yay!

You'll need to activate the End portal by filling the empty frames with eyes of ender. Add a sticker of a silverfish to the info card to learn all about it.

SILVERFISH

HOSTILITY	6	HEALTH	8
ATTACK	1	XP	5
DROPS		NOTHING	

ℹ️ Silverfish are so small that they'll sink into soul sand and suffocate.

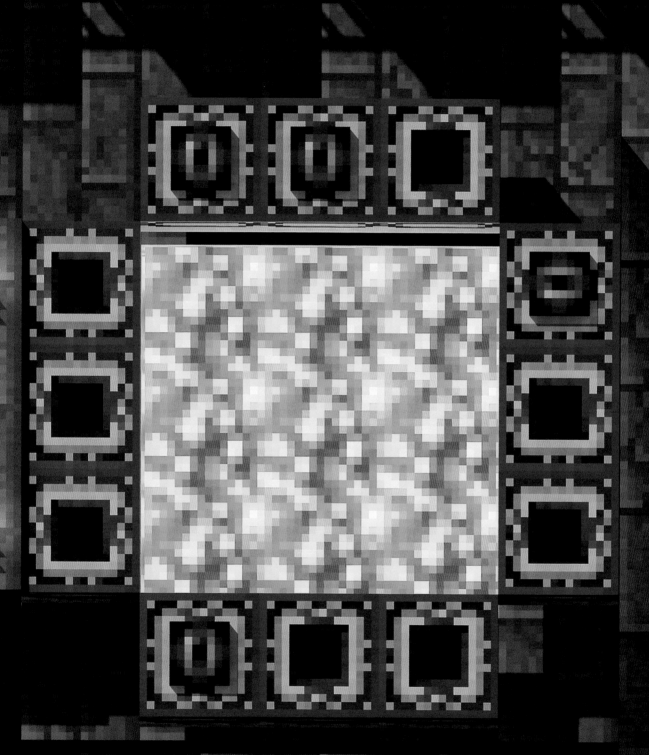

THE END

You've finally made it to the End's main island. There's not much on the island except for endermen and the dreaded ender dragon.

It's time to make a plan – build an emergency shelter to keep you safe while you decide on your next move, and add some endermen into the scene.

PODIUM

There's a strange podium in the middle of the island, made from bedrock. The dragon seems to be very protective of it …

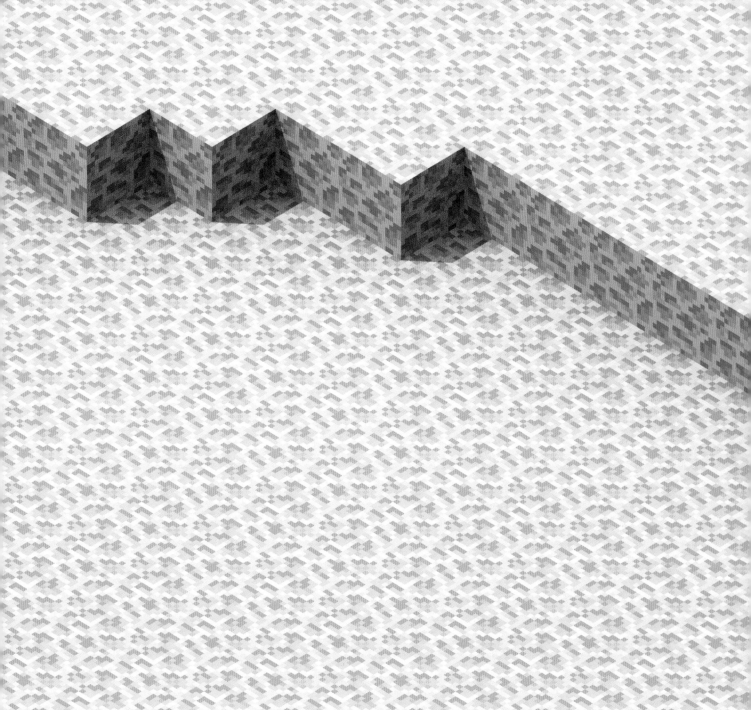

DRAGON FIGHT

COMBAT
WITH SCOUT

You'll need nerves of steel to defeat the ender dragon. I'm just the person to help you win the fiercest battle of your life.

Add yourself into the scene, then complete the info boxes with the correct stickers to learn how to defeat Minecraft's deadliest boss mob.

DRAGON EGG

The dragon egg is a trophy that appears on the podium when you defeat the ender dragon. It can't be mined with a tool – you'll need to use a piston to push it onto a solid block before you can collect it.

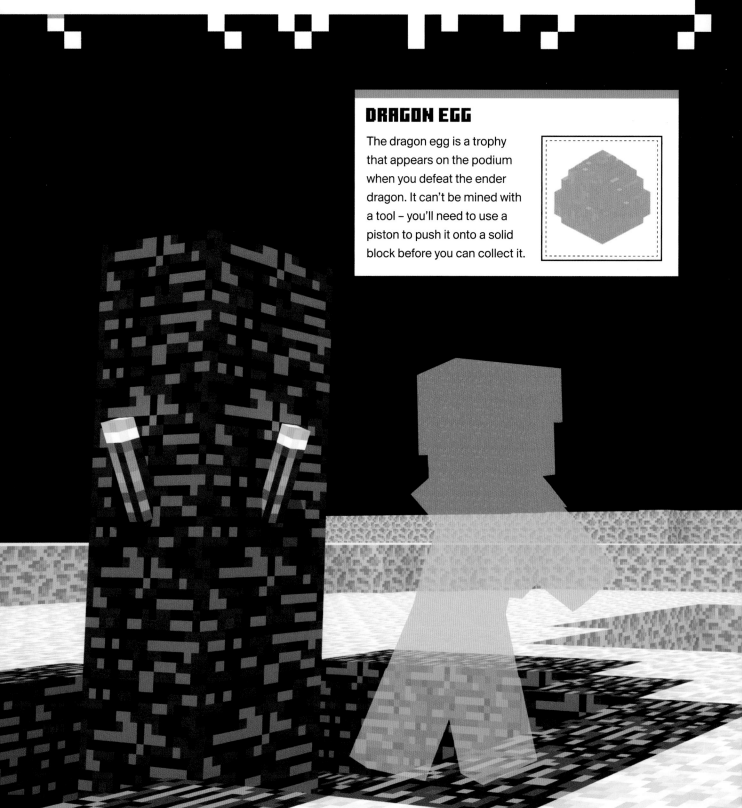

BED

Beds explode if you try to use them in the End, which means they can be used as weapons against the dragon. Be careful you don't blow yourself up too, though!

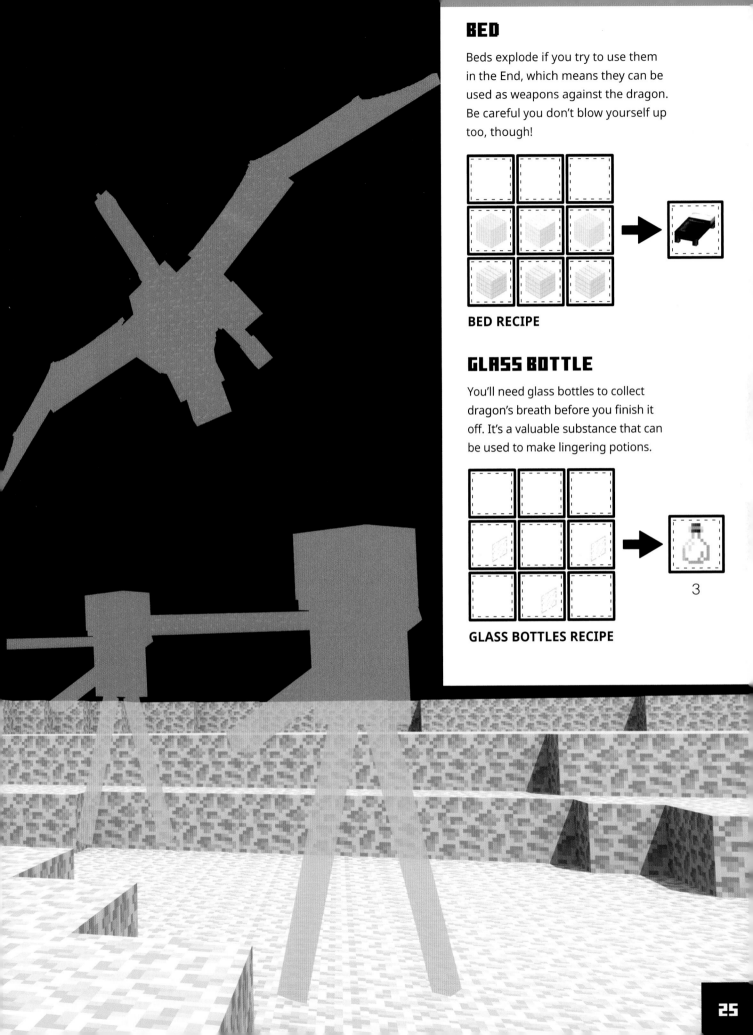

BED RECIPE

GLASS BOTTLE

You'll need glass bottles to collect dragon's breath before you finish it off. It's a valuable substance that can be used to make lingering potions.

3

GLASS BOTTLES RECIPE

THE END CITY

EXPLORING
WITH BEAR

You may have defeated the dragon, but that doesn't mean you can relax. If you travel to an End city on the outer islands you'll need to be very careful.

Find stickers for each of the things you'll see in an End city and learn more about them.

END SHIP

These floating ships are where you'll find elytra – wings that allow you to glide in Survival mode. There's also a dragon head at the end of the ship – this is the only place you'll find one.

DRAGON HEAD

ELYTRA

CHORUS FRUIT

CHORUS PLANT

These towering purple structures are the only plants that grow on the outer islands. They drop chorus fruit when mined, which can be eaten or cooked to make popped chorus fruit.

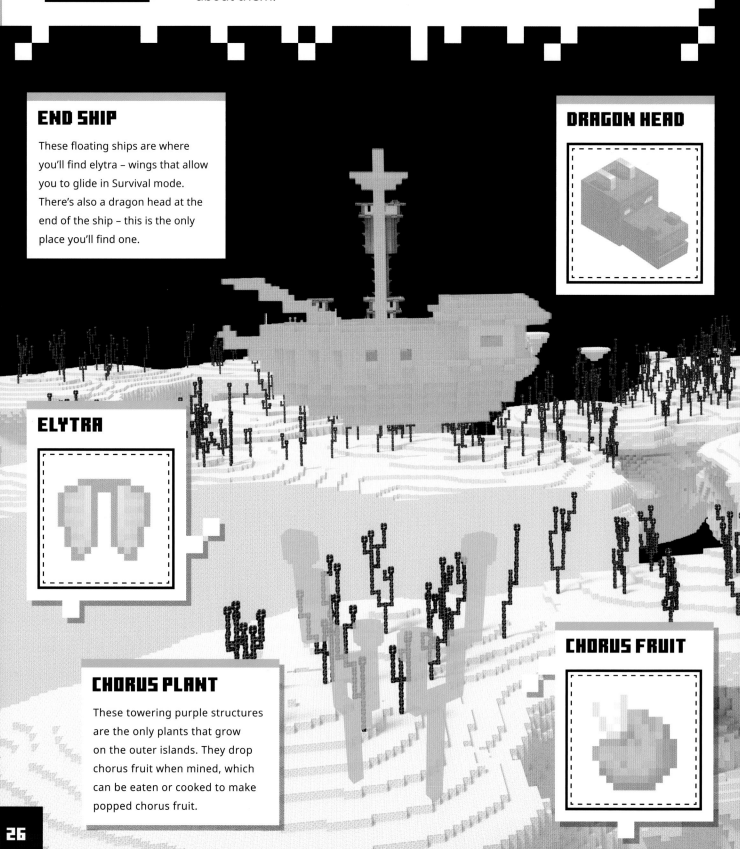

TOWER

The city is made up of several towers built from End stone and purpur blocks. You'll find hostile creatures called shulkers living inside these towers, so be very careful.

SHULKER SKIRMISH

Whilst exploring the End city you spot a shulker. You've heard about these creatures, but never faced one before.

Find some stickers on your sticker sheet to complete the story of your skirmish with the shulker.

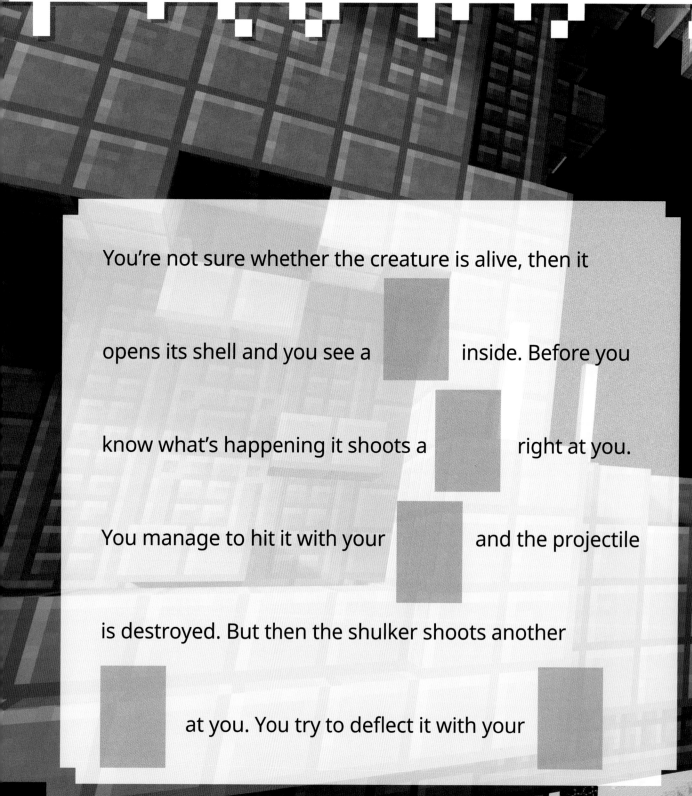

You're not sure whether the creature is alive, then it

opens its shell and you see a   inside. Before you

know what's happening it shoots a   right at you.

You manage to hit it with your   and the projectile

is destroyed. But then the shulker shoots another

              at you. You try to deflect it with your

but you're not quick enough and it hits you. You begin to

float up into the air. You search your inventory for

something to stop it, and find a   . You're not sure

whether it will work, but you drink the   anyway.

To your relief, you stop floating upwards. You're only a

little way above the ground, so you don't take much

damage when you fall back to earth. You land right next

to the shulker and hit it with your   . Defeated, it

falls over and drops a   . You're not quite sure

what this strange object does, but it better be good!

HOME SWEET HOME

Congratulations – you've conquered all three of Minecraft's dimensions! Now you can travel back and forth to explore whenever you like.

Use stickers to build a base on the main island, so you'll always have a safe place to come back to.

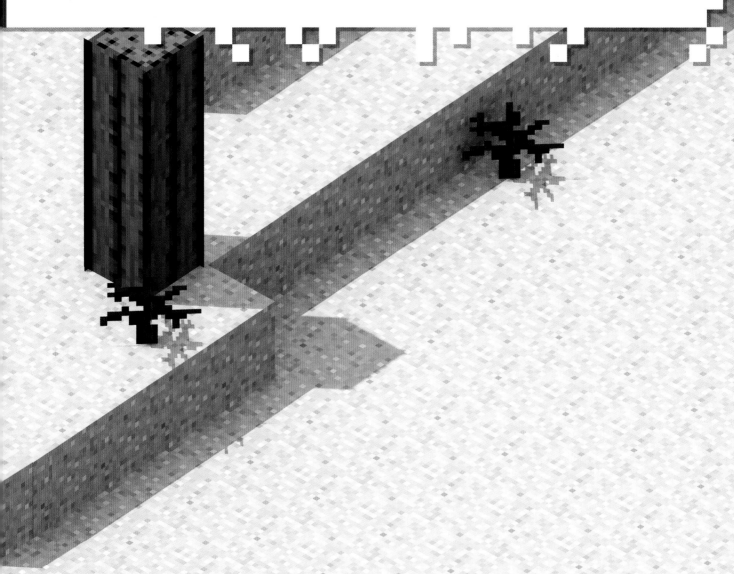

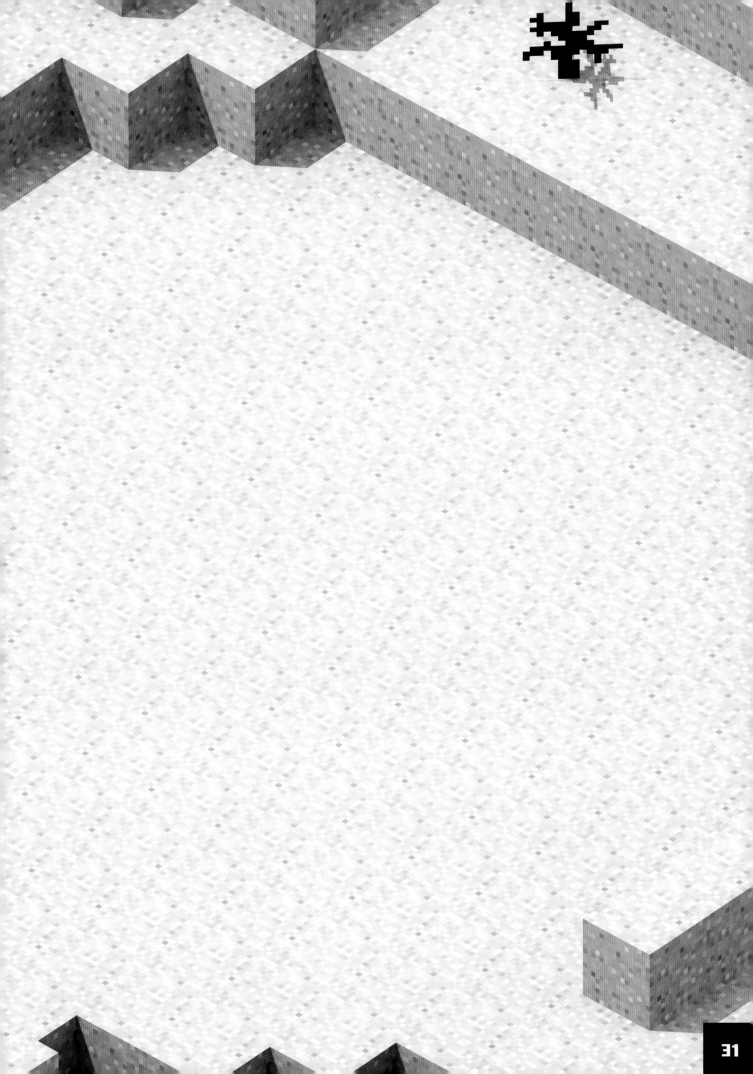

ELYTRA ACE

SURVIVAL
WITH BEAR

As the proud owner of a shiny new set of elytra, survival in all dimensions just got a lot easier. The hostile mobs will never catch you now.

Add Steve into the scene as he demonstrates how to use the elytra.

ANSWERS

Pages 6-7:

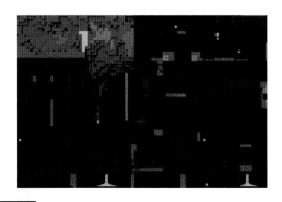

Pages 12-13:

1. Netherrack
2. Glowstone dust
3. Soul sand
4. Nether brick
5. Magma block
6. Nether quartz

Pages 16-17:

Desert

Pages 18-19:

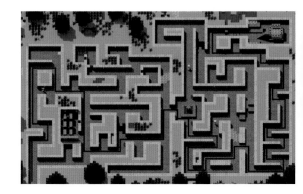

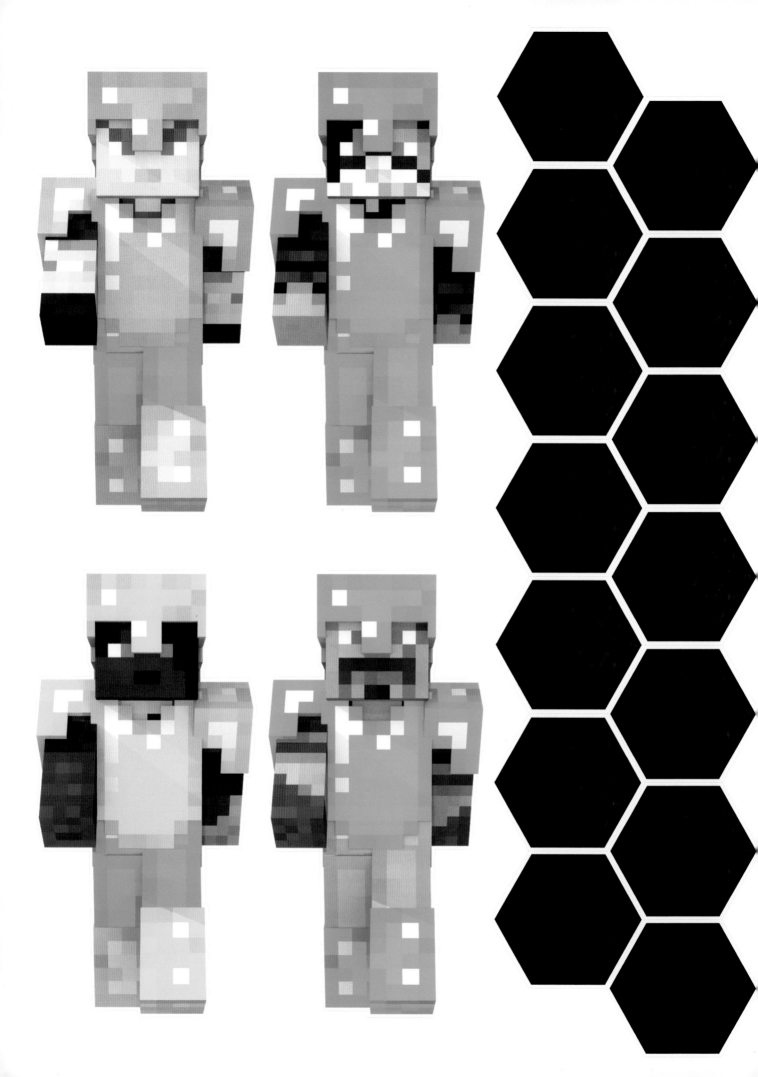

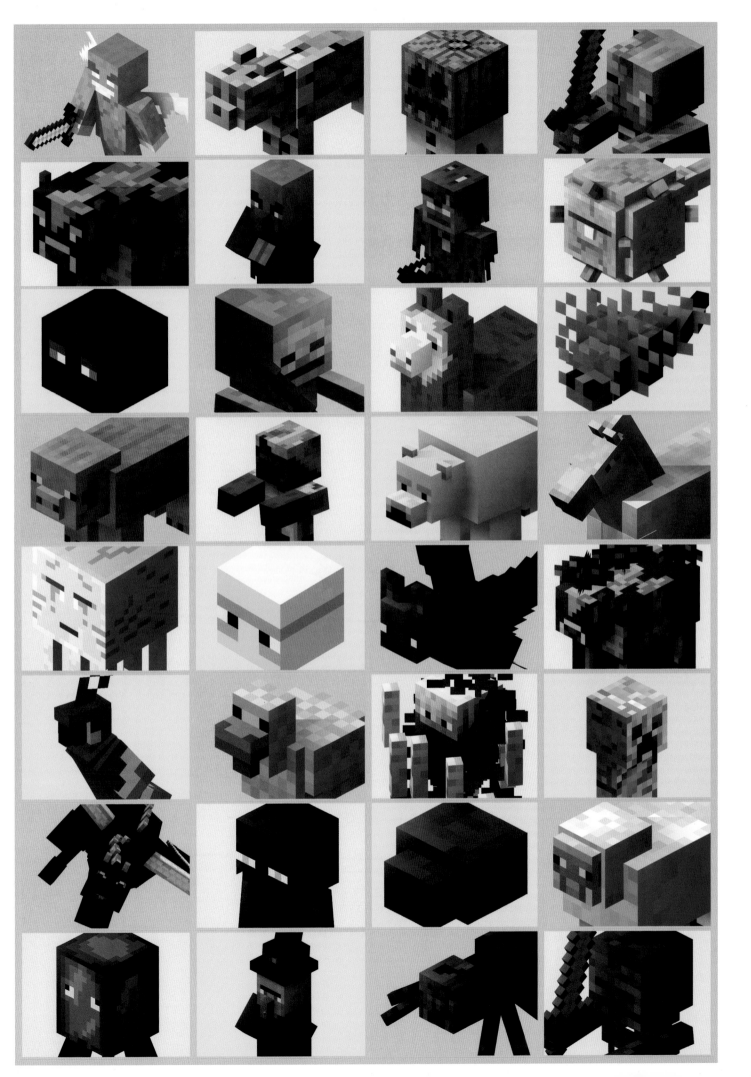

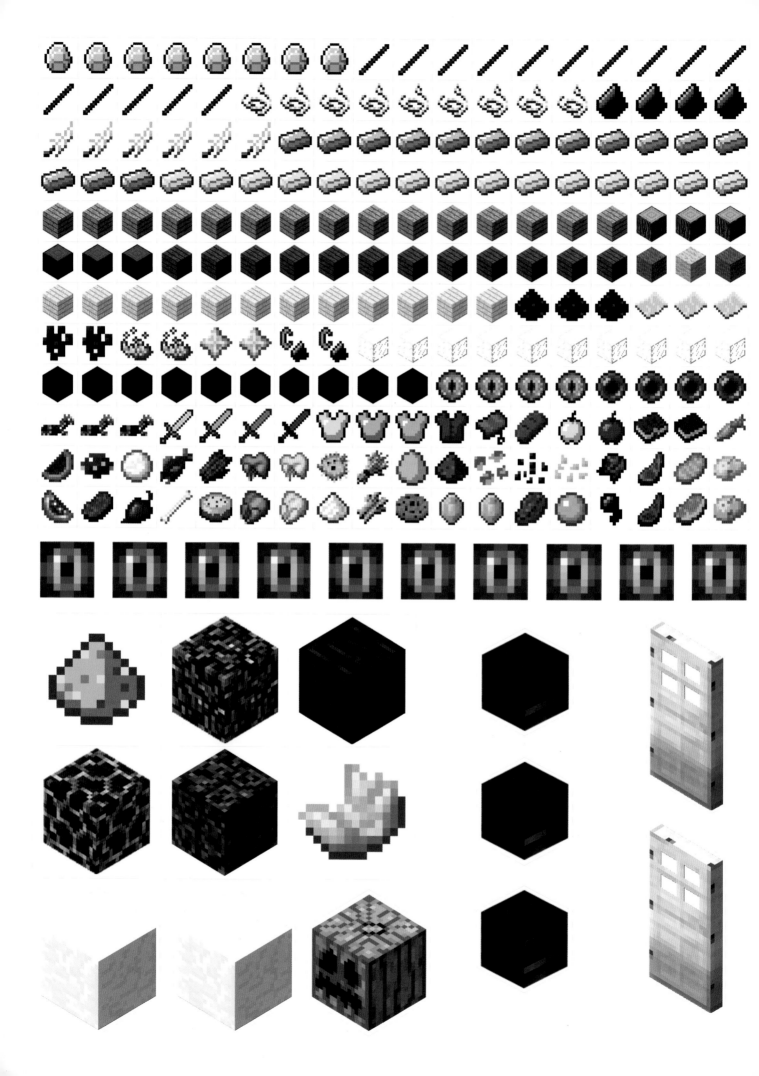

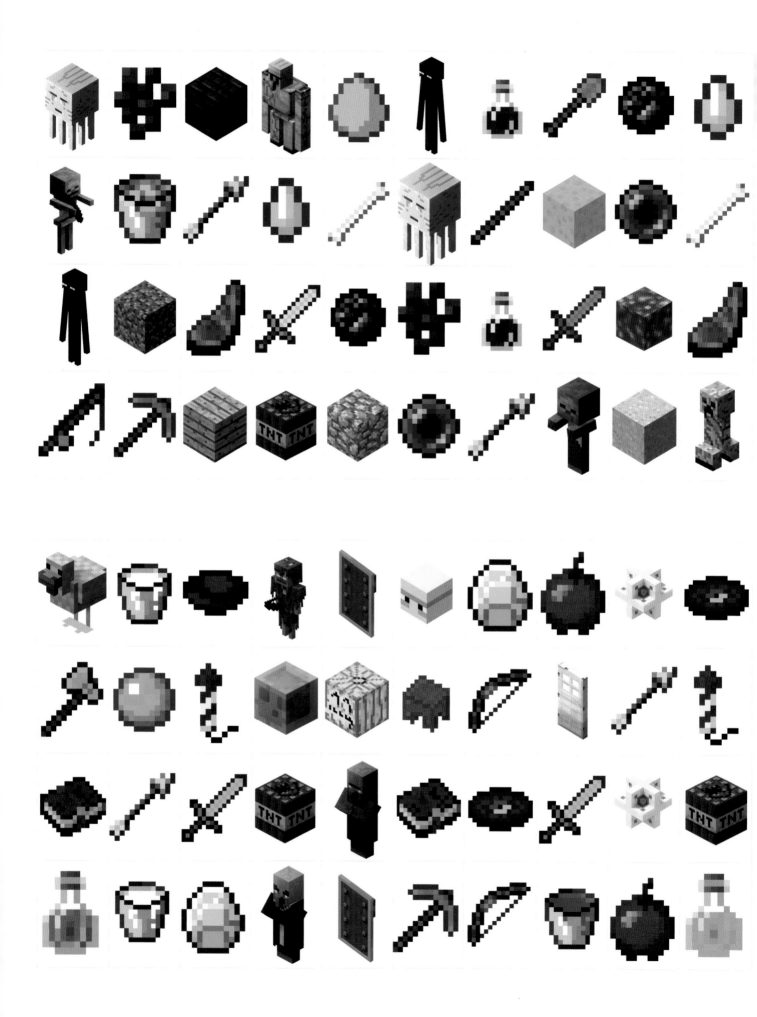

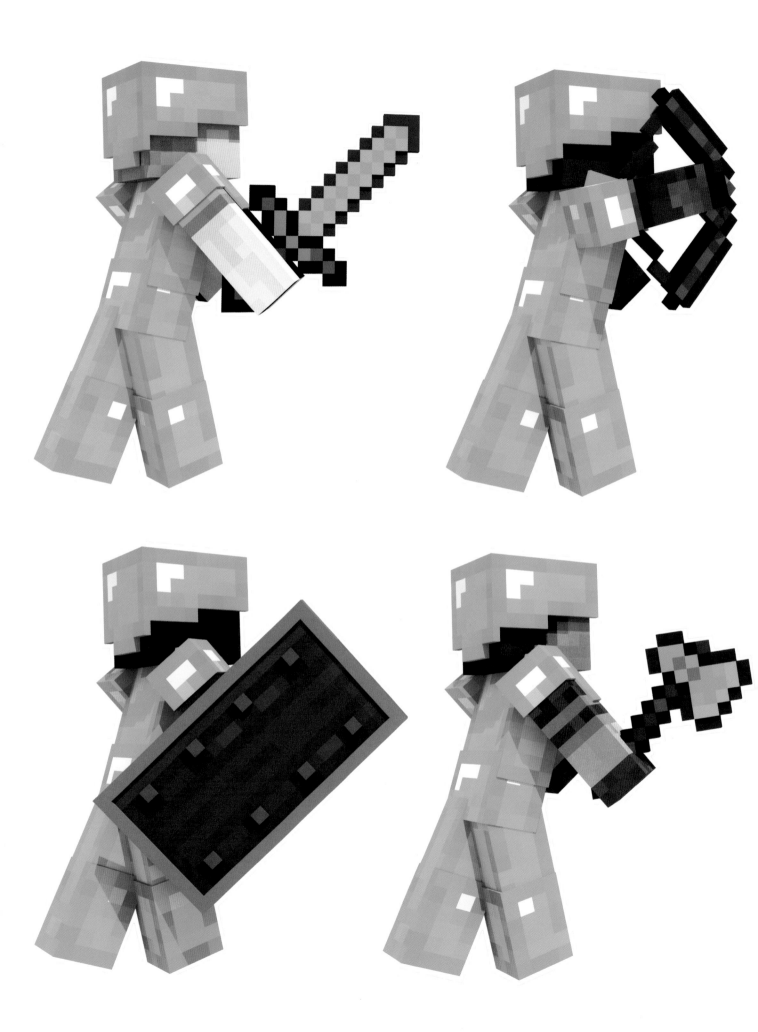

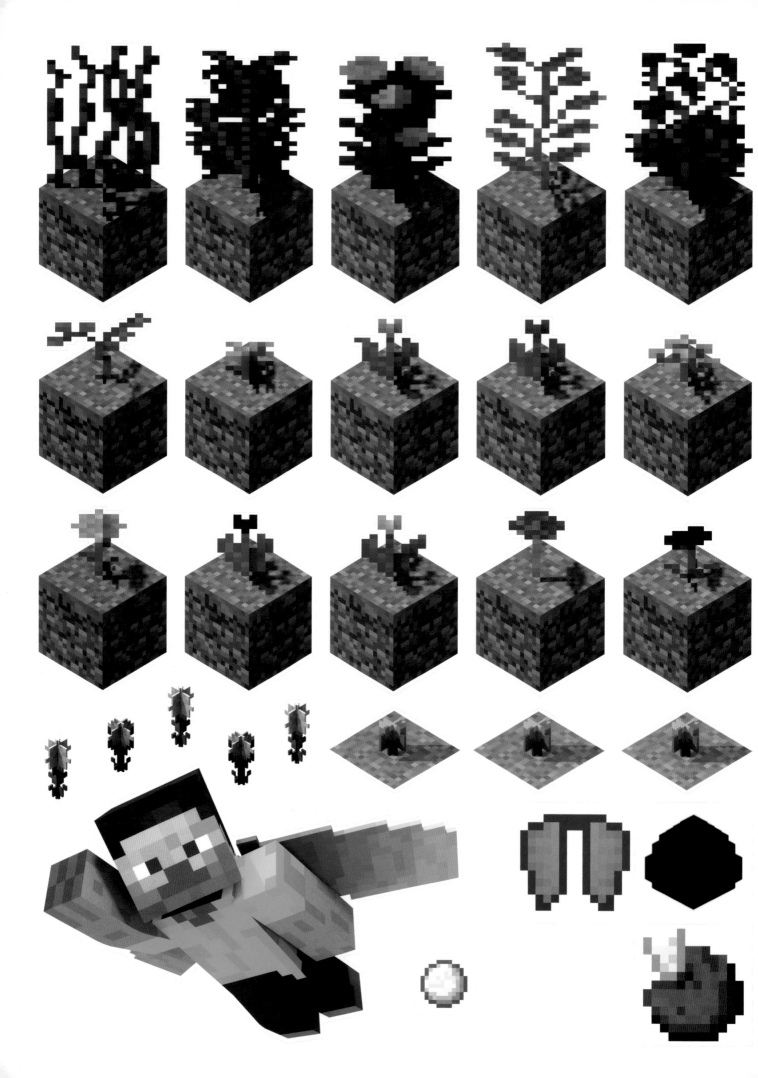